A House To Let

Mrs. Molesworth

Nabu Public Domain Reprints:

You are holding a reproduction of an original work published before 1923 that is in the public domain in the United States of America, and possibly other countries. You may freely copy and distribute this work as no entity (individual or corporate) has a copyright on the body of the work. This book may contain prior copyright references, and library stamps (as most of these works were scanned from library copies). These have been scanned and retained as part of the historical artifact.

This book may have occasional imperfections such as missing or blurred pages, poor pictures, errant marks, etc. that were either part of the original artifact, or were introduced by the scanning process. We believe this work is culturally important, and despite the imperfections, have elected to bring it back into print as part of our continuing commitment to the preservation of printed works worldwide. We appreciate your understanding of the imperfections in the preservation process, and hope you enjoy this valuable book.

A HOUSE TO LET.

BY

MRS. MOLESWORTH,

Author of "Carrots," "Two Little Waifs," "Little Miss Peggy," &c.

"WE WILL NOT DESERT NUMBER NINE."

LONDON:
SOCIETY FOR PROMOTING CHRISTIAN KNOWLEDGE,
NORTHUMBERLAND AVENUE, W.C.; 43 QUEEN VICTORIA STREET.
BRIGHTON: 135 NORTH STREET.
NEW YORK: E. & J. B. YOUNG & CO.

Richard Clay and Sons, Limited,
London and Bungay.

CONTENTS.

	PAGE
CHAPTER I.	
A Flitting	5
CHAPTER II.	
Poppy	13
CHAPTER III.	
Flip's Appeal	20
CHAPTER IV.	
Castles in the Air	28
CHAPTER V.	
The Birthday Wish	36
CHAPTER VI.	
Fairyland	44
CHAPTER VII.	
A Mouse Conclave	52
CHAPTER VIII.	
Poppy Gives and Takes Advice	60
CHAPTER IX.	
Bad News	67
CHAPTER X.	
Delia's Big Sister	75
CHAPTER XI.	
Almost Too Good to be True	83
CHAPTER XII.	
Delia's Dream	90

A HOUSE TO LET.

CHAPTER I.

A FLITTING.

SOMETHING was going to happen at No. 9. That was clear. The children behind the bars of the high-up nursery windows across the street could have told the most, I dare say. For one or two of them had had colds and had not been allowed to go out for a week or so, and their best amusement had been to watch the doings of their opposite neighbours. They could have told you how the old lady and gentleman had made two or three short journeys this winter, in spite of the cold, staying away a night or so only, they who for more years than the children certainly could remember had made but one annual flitting to the seaside every autumn. And now when a couple of cabs, so loaded with luggage inside and out that the old gentleman's valet and the old lady's maid could scarcely find room in either, had driven away from the door from which a moment before the neat brougham had started with the old people themselves, the children knew all about it.

"They've left for good now," said Bessie, who being a girl, of course jumped to conclusions much quicker than Jack, who though he was older and bigger, laboured, poor fellow, under the disadvantage of being only a boy. It wasn't exactly his fault, to be sure; still he was never allowed to forget it, for there were three sisters "on the top of him," as Bessie said, and the

"They've left for good now"

two brothers who came "behind her" were too small to be good for much in the way of backing him up. He was really "Jack in the middle;" but long ago it had been decided in this family that there were to be *two* "Jacks in the middle," even though it put it all rather crooked. For Bessie and he were so much nearer each other in age than they were near the big sisters on the one hand, or the little brothers on the other, that it would have been absurd to "count ourselves any other way," said all of them. And the arrangement was very well carried out. Jack and Bessie kept together faithfully. They did everything together, even to getting into long division and having the measles. And this winter they had got bad colds together, which was rather a good plan, as they could stay in the same room, and have the same hot gruel at night and the same medicine marked "three times a day." They were sensible children, you see. I call it very sensible to have chosen the very time for their bad colds when there was a removal going on at No. 9 opposite.

For that was the meaning of the unusual journeys and general excitement, as Bessie had guessed.

"They've left for good now," she said. "Poor old lady and gentleman. It makes me rather sad—doesn't it you, Jack?—to think we'll never see them again? In a day or two, you'll see, there'll come two or three great big vans and a lot of men, and all the furniture'll be carried out and packed into the vans and there'll be 'A house to let' opposite, Jack."

Jack listened admiringly. Bessie was only seven, and he was eight and a half. He felt that she was far forwarder for her age than he. But he was a nice boy—he didn't feel jealous—it was only fair for girls to have *something* better than boys, for it must be very sad never to be able to look forward to having Eton jackets and trousers, or boots with nails in, or football flannels like their big cousin D'Arcy. From which you will see that all the wholesome snubbing of Flora and Pleasance and Agnes had fallen on rather stony ground. Jack wouldn't have *not* been a boy, not for—oh, I can't find any strong enough words to say for it!

"I hope it won't be 'A house to let' for long," he replied. "Can't you guess about that too, Bessie? I should like new people to come at once, while we're not doing lessons. It would be fun to see the furniture all going in, and to watch to see what they were like."

But Bessie wasn't enough of a gipsy to predict any more. She was right enough so far—the big vans came and the furniture was all carried out and the street was left very messy-looking in front of No. 9 for a day or two, with bits of straw and paper and ends of string fluttering about. The last person to come out was the old gentleman and lady's old cook, who had stayed behind to see that all was right. She wasn't going to be their cook any more, for she was getting too old. And she wiped her eyes rather sadly as she shut-to the area gate for the last time, and out of the covered basket which she carried on her arm there came a plaintive mew of sympathy, for the old cook was taking the old lady's old cat away with her.

"She'll be company for you," the old lady had said kindly, "and she'd never take to country ways. You must bring her to see us when you come to spend a day though."

For the old gentleman and lady had taken a house some way out of town. They were getting too stiff for London stairs, they said, and they wanted a garden to stroll about in.

Jack and Bessie had not been the only—people I was going to say, but that would not do—*ones*, I'll say for the present, to watch with interest the signs of a removal from No. 9. There was a whole family even more interested in it than the two children opposite.

And on the evening of the day which saw the departure of the old cook and the old cat, the excitement of this family reached its height.

"It's true, it's all true—our best hopes are fulfilled. Ah my poor heart! It is palpitating with emotion. I shall never again be the—the mouse I was, I fear, my beloved Mrs. Bright-eyes. What I have gone through of late since our little ones have been old enough to run about alone, no one knows."

And Mr. Bright-eyes smoothed his ruffled fur with his paws—for a mouse's fur *can* be rubbed the wrong way, though you mightn't think it—and looked up to his plump little wife for sympathy.

"My poor dear," she said feelingly, "I can't bear to think of it. But you speak of good news—can it be—is it possible that the—the unmentionable one—is gone? Has she over-eaten herself—has her hideous voice at last worn out some neighbour's patience? Why if *I* were a human being I would not have endured her a single night! But alas! *such* good news is not to be hoped for."

"I beg your pardon, my love. Our fiendish enemy, the enemy of our race, is, I may take upon myself to say, still in the land of the living, but she will never trouble *us* more. I have just from a hole in the kitchen cupboard watched her departure—her final departure, Mrs. Bright-eyes, in a basket on the cook's arm. And as they left the kitchen, cook looked round and said, 'So it's good-bye to the old place at last for you and me, pussy.' At which *she*, the nameless one, mewed. 'And even for your sake, pussy,' continued the deluded creature, 'I cannot hope for mice in our new home. For they are the most destructivest and forage-ousist pests as never was. They may have it all their own way here now howsome-never for all I cares.' And with that she shut the door, sending my poor heart pit-a-pat, and I darted home to tell you. But the emotion is too much for me. Have you a morsel of something at hand? I could—I think I could swallow a crumb of

The DEPARTURE OF THE UNMENTIONABLE ONE

sponge-cake—there was some at afternoon-tea as usual, I suppose? 'Twas you who were in the drawing-room yesterday."

"You forget, my love—there has been no sponge-cake since the old lady left. That mean creature, the cook, had nothing but toast for her tea. However there was some gingerbread left in the sideboard. I brought some pieces home. You will find it not so bad."

Mr & Mrs. Bright-eyes

CHAPTER II.

POPPY.

MRS. BRIGHT-EYES handed the gingerbread crumbs to her husband. He thanked her politely. "I am not difficult to please, my love," he remarked as he munched it. "Better by far, I always say, the poorest fare if in peace and security. I *could* even eat bread and cheese if we were put to it."

"And you think the coast is really clear?" said Mrs. Bright-eyes anxiously.

"I feel sure of it," he replied. "This afternoon I shall reconnoitre again, and if all is right the children may accompany us on a stroll round the kitchen, dear things. How often they have wished to visit it! We shall be able to introduce them to all our pet haunts, and show them the spots where you and I wandered in our sentimental days. The pastry cupboard, the shelf where stand the jars of dripping, the sugar canister! Ah, what sweet memories are mingled with them all—and to think we can now visit them as often as we choose! This day is a reward for all our sufferings."

THE DRIPPING JAR WAS EMPTY—

But Mr. Bright-eyes' jubilation was rather damped, when, accompanied by his promising family, he had made the proposed tour. The pastry cupboard was empty; of the jars of dripping there remained but one, containing but a mere smearing; the sugar canister had bodily disappeared! Papa and Mamma Bright-eyes looked rather blank.

"What a mean revenge!" they said to each other.

The young Bright-eyes were not disconcerted. They found plenty to amuse them—it was great fun to rush about the kitchen, and in their ignorance they did not perceive the bareness of the land. There were still crumbs here and there and some small fragments of cheese not to be despised, though their Papa looked down upon it as most plebeian food for mice of quality. And he was too shocked and startled by the state of things to rebuke them for eating anything they found.

"Take comfort, my love," said his wife. "We are still a long way from starvation. There is a good deal of sawdust and bran in the wine-cellar, there are some remains of candle-ends in the kitchen dresser, and even the scraps of oilcloth about the passages are not to be despised in case of necessity."

But Papa Bright-eyes nearly fainted at her words. I am afraid he was something of a gourmand.

"Hush, hush, my love," he whispered, "you mean well, but your suggestions are terrible. Could one have believed that human spite would have gone so far? Could one have believed in such ingenuity of cruelty? The nameless one has left us, it is true, but only to a fate almost as cruel as her claws—to slow starvation. We must emigrate, my love, we must emigrate!"

"To a country where no nameless ones are to be found, then, I hope," said Mrs. Bright-eyes. "For my part I'd rather make the best of sawdust and oilcloth, and even a nibble at wall-paper now and then, than risk coming across any of that lot, I must say."

But as a week or two passed, and the last scraps of cheese had disappeared, and mouldy bran grew rather monotonous fare, even Mamma Bright-eyes began to urge upon her husband the desirability of a voyage of discovery into one of the neighbouring houses which were not to let. And there is no knowing what the unfortunate family might not have been driven to, had not an unexpected event happened.

Till now the house had been left empty. The old gentleman and lady were in some ways a little too economically inclined, and they had felt so sure of finding tenants or purchasers at once that they had not thought it necessary to put in a caretaker. But it was a bad season for letting or selling houses, and at last their agent persuaded them to put some one in charge who could "keep the dust down" and answer any inquiries that might be made at the door. So one morning Jack and Bessie, whose colds were quite gone by this time, on coming in from their usual walk, were very much surprised as they passed No. 9 to see a little girl standing at the area gate, looking up and down the street with eager eyes. She was a pleasant-faced child, with short black hair, bright dark eyes and rosy cheeks, and her pinafore, though threadbare in some places and darned in others, was clean.

Bessie, who was of a sociable disposition and not troubled with shyness, stopped short at sight of the little maiden and looked at her inquiringly. The nurses and the two little brothers were some way down the street, coming along more slowly. A smile came over the rosy face, and to Bessie this smile was irresistible.

"Are you—have you come to live here?" she added.

"Please'm, yes'm," replied the child promptly. "Mother and me's a-caretaking, but mother's out charing. She said as how I might stand 'ere to take the air a bit—it's beautiful air it is, Miss, in this 'ere street," she burst out enthusiastically, "but as how I mustn't step outside the gate. It isn't every day as mother's charing—just permiscous-like, you see."

"Are you very dull alone?" asked Bessie sympathizingly. She could not by any means understand all that the child said, but this question seemed safe ground.

"Bless you, no, Miss. It's a lovely house—it is a pleasure to sweep the rooms. And there's mice, Miss, as'd make you die with laughing. They seem half starved, they're so uncommon hungry. They'll eat the crumbs and we as close as close. I never did see such mice."

"How *very* nice," exclaimed Bessie feelingly. "Jack, do you hear? I wish I could see them. We'll talk to you again another day, little girl, but we must run in now. That's our house opposite."

"That's our nursery window—the one with the bars, do you see?" added Jack, eager to put in a word.

"You may look up there and we'll nod to you," said Bessie condescendingly. "What's your name?"

"It was great fun to rush about"

"Please'm, Poppy'm. Leastways I'm called Poppy, but S'lina Mary's my proper name?"

"Sleener-mary, what a queer name! I like Poppy better. We'll call you Poppy," said Bessie, as she and Jack ran off.

CHAPTER III.

FLIP'S APPEAL.

MASTER FLIP

WHEN Poppy had had air enough and staring up and down the street enough, she retired into the kitchen. It was dinner time by now. She got out a plate with a bit of cold boiled bacon, and managed cleverly enough, by the aid of a shovel, to warm up a roast potato over from last night's supper. And then she sat down to enjoy this unusually good dinner, as happy as a queen. Had she not every reason to be happy? No more question of rent—a nice bit of fire, a good dinner, mother's face cheerier than it had been since the long ago golden days, remembered by little Poppy but as in a dream, when "father" was alive and earning good wages.

The smell of the bacon and hot potato skin reached other nostrils besides Poppy's. Father Bright-eyes was on the watch. Things had been coming to a very bad pass with him and his family the last few days, and hunger makes brave. Besides, Poppy was far less alarming than a certain not-to-be-named personage. As she slowly finished the last scraps of her dinner, a slight, very slight sound behind her made her look round, and the long tail of Papa Bright-eyes caught her glance ere he whisked it after him down the hole in the corner of the cupboard.

"Ah, there you are, mousey," said the little girl, "don't be afraid, poor dear. I'm not a-going to hurt you. And I've left some nice crumbs of potato skin and a bit of bacon rind for you. See there, I'll put it down in front of the 'earth, so as you can be nice and warm while you eats it. And I'm just a-going to take a nap, so I'll not even see as you're there. You've no call to be afraid—go and fetch all the family if you please. We've no cat—mother and me, we don't hold with cats."

Then Poppy curled herself up in mother's big old arm-chair, the one comfortable piece of furniture they possessed, and pretended to go to sleep, all out of kindness to Bright-eyes and his belongings. She lay so still that when Bright-eyes peeped out again he ventured to come out some way further; still the

AS HAPPY AS A QUEEN

little figure in the big chair was motionless; he peeped up at her, and the scrap of bacon rind smelt *so* good that hunger overcame prudence, and in another minute he was dining most comfortably close to the fire where Poppy had placed the crumbs. It was long since he had had so good a meal, but he would not keep it all for himself. Back to the cupboard he flitted, returning in a moment with Mrs. Bright-eyes and the four small ones. There was not very much dinner for them after all, but what there was tasted very good, and not the tiniest crumb was left when they had finished.

All this time Poppy was peeping at them through her fingers, though she took care to keep perfectly still.

"One, two, three, four," she counted, "oh what fun! *Six* little mice. My! mustn't they just be hungry to come out so bold—poor little mice. I wish I'd more to give you. I'll try and save a scrap or two of my supper. Wouldn't the young lady and gentleman like to see them? That little fellow with the funny twist in his tail is the sharpest of all—how he does flash about! I wonder if they won't get to know me quite well once they sees I'm not a-going to hurt 'em."

She moved her foot a very little, just to try. In an instant, as if by magic, the whole six had disappeared—Poppy could almost have fancied it a dream that they had been there at all!

She went up the area steps again when she had "washed up," as she called it, though, as the things consisted only of one plate and a knife and fork, it was not a long process. There was the hearth to sweep up however, and a lump of coal to be carefully placed so that it would last till mother came in, and tea had to be got ready; so Poppy felt herself quite a housekeeper. She glanced at the opposite house, but there were no faces at the nursery window; for just then Jack and Bessie were more profitably occupied in discussing their dinner. So Poppy got out her knitting when she came in again, and settled herself in the big arm-chair, wondering how many rounds of her stocking she would be able to get done before mother came home. And then a queer thing happened. A very, *very* soft sound made her look, not up, but down, for the sound came from below. There, just where her feet would have come to had her legs been longer, stood a mouse—a very small one, with a slight twist at the end of his long tail. He lifted his two front paws much as a squirrel does when he is holding a nut to nibble, only poor mousey had no nut.

"Poppy," he said in a clear squeaky voice, "I have crept out all of myself to speak to you. I am sure you are good and kind. We have been in great trouble—we have been nearly starving, and my Papa and Mamma had almost made up their minds to emigrate" (here the mouse's feelings choked his voice for a moment), "when you came. Your goodness in giving us our dinner to-day has made them think better of it.

FLIP'S APPEAL.

May we trust to you to take care of us? Will you promise never, never to—to—"

"To set a cat on you?" said Poppy. But a faint squeal from the mouse startled her.

"Don't—don't, I beg of you—don't say the word—I shall die if you say it again."

"Well then, I won't," said Poppy good-naturedly. "And I'll promise you no one shall hurt you, so long as you don't do no mischief to our things. And I'll give you all the scraps I can, though they won't be much. Mother and me's poor folk though we do live in a fine house—we're only caretaking you see."

"Thank you, Poppy," said the mouse. "I shall carry the good news home. You may trust us to do no mischief. We have been very well brought up, I assure you. Thank you very much," and he was flitting away when Poppy stopped him.

"What's your name, mousey?" she said.

"Flip," he replied. "I am the eldest of the family. You may know me by the twist in my tail. In our family the eldest son is always distinguished by this graceful twist. We are very proud of it. Good evening, Poppy."

He darted off—but as he went, his long tail touched her feet. Poppy jumped up—had she been asleep? One of her knitting needles had dropped out and was sticking between her slipper and her stocking. How provoking! Several stitches had slipped—she had to work hard to finish the rounds she had set herself before mother came home. How very funny it was about Flip! Could it have been a dream only? Any way *she* would keep her promise.

CHAPTER IV.

CASTLES IN THE AIR.

WHEN Jack and Bessie came into the day-nursery for their breakfast the next morning they ran to the window to look out. Yes, there at the top of the area steps, looking up and down the street, just like the day before, stood Poppy. It was a bright morning, though rather chilly—the sun was in Poppy's eyes, and she did not see the two faces pressed against the window pane, till a tinkling sort of knocking made her look up. Jack was drumming on the glass with a tin trumpet. Then Poppy's face broke out in smiles. She nodded and they nodded. Next a sudden idea struck her. She held out all the fingers of one hand and the forefinger of the other, bobbing them down in turns to show she was counting.

"One, two, three, four, five, six," she said aloud, as if her voice could possibly have reached them.

"What can she mean?" said Bessie, "she keeps counting up to six, do you see, Jack? I'll try to make her understand that we'll talk to her again when we go out." And a series of very funny signs and pointings ensued, which unfortunately Poppy could *not* understand at all.

But she kept her eye on the opposite house all the morning, and she was at her post when at last the door opened and the two children ran out. The nurses were getting the little ones down stairs and there was always some delay with the perambulator, so Jack and Bessie had time for a word or two.

"What *were* you counting on your fingers this morning, Poppy?" asked Bessie.

"It were the mice, Miss. You would have laughed. There's

six on 'em, all six at onst. You never did see nothing so funny. And I've promised as I'll give 'em scraps—poor things, they've been all but starved."

"What were you counting on your fingers,?"

"You've promised," repeated Bessie. "But how could you promise *mice* anything?"

Poppy got rather red.

"Oh, Miss, don't you laugh at me now, but p'r'aps I were dreaming. All the same I promised," and she related Flip's visit the evening before.

Jack and Bessie were delighted. They would have stayed talking to Poppy for some time longer, had not a bumping, jerking sound across the street announced the exit of the perambulator. So off they flew. But Poppy's communications gave them plenty to chatter about to each other that morning. *Was* it a dream, or could it be that mice could *sometimes* speak?

From this time forward not many days passed on which they did not manage to have a little conversation with Poppy. Their nurse noticed her standing at the gate once or twice but without paying particular attention, and as the child bobbed a courtesy and a pleasant good morning, she was quite satisfied when Bessie spoke of her as "the caretaker's little girl opposite." Not that Jack and Bessie had the least idea of concealing their acquaintance with Poppy. If any one had asked about it they would have told all there was to tell, but no one happened to do so. Their mother was even more busy than usual just then, as the big sisters were without a governess, and she had herself to help them in preparing their lessons for their various masters.

Poppy's mother seemed to be in great request just then. "It never rains but it pours," says the proverb, and now that she was living rent free she had more "charing" than during all the past hard winter. When she came home in the evening she was often too tired to tell her little daughter the stories that had always been the child's favourites—of "when poor father was alive and we lived in the country." "The country" was Poppy's fairyland; she had never seen it that she could remember, she tried to picture it to herself from her mother's descriptions, to be sure, but still, as the good woman told her, "no words could give the *feel* of it." And they used to build castles in the air together of a day when they should have saved enough to go for some hours by one of the cheap excursions they saw posters about at the railway stations, "right into the real country."

But lately the story-telling had been on Poppy's side much more than on her mother's. The poor woman was often so tired now that she liked better to listen than to talk, and Poppy was very pleased to retail all her conversations with Jack and Bessie, and she was also very fond of chattering to her mother about Flip and his brothers and sisters.

"What a fancy the child has, to be sure," her mother would say with a smile. "How I do wish I could show you some of the pretty wild creatures as lives in the woods! The squirrels with

FATHER BRIGHT-EYES WAS PEEPING OUT,

their long tails, and the rabbits a-scuttling about, and the birds. When I was as little as you, Poppy, I used to know 'em all by sight and by sound you might say—you've no notion what a lot of kinds of birds there was down our way."

"Wouldn't I like to see them!" said Poppy. "I do like alive things, mother. I'd rather a deal have the mice running about than nothing stirring when you're out. And I do believe as the little one with the twisty tail as I was telling you of, is getting to know me. I always put some crumbs for 'em at the same place, and now they'll come close to my foot."

"I can't say as I'm partial to mice," said Poppy's mother. "Still, I don't suppose they can do much harm here in this empty house. If I thought they were mischievous, Poppy, I'd have to get a cat."

"Oh, mother," almost screamed Poppy, "you'd never go for to do that! They'll do no mischief—you may be sure. Flip promised—you remember, mother, I told you. And if it was a dream, there's dreams as is true. Oh, mother, you'll never get a cat."

Poppy looked ready to cry. But her mother comforted her by saying she had no wish to get a cat; "cats was great worries, and took a deal of milk," there was no need for Poppy to work herself up.

Some one else was very glad to hear what Poppy's mother said. Father Bright-eyes was peeping out of the cupboard, listening.

Things had been better of late, for though the fare was certainly not as good as in the old days, the scraps which Poppy provided were much to be preferred to sawdust and oilcloth. And then even if there were not much, at least it could be eaten in peace!

"WOULDN'T I LIKE TO SEE THEM!"
SAID POPPY.

CHAPTER V.

THE BIRTHDAY WISH.

"I AM REALLY IN A POSITION TO ADVISE YOU,"

"WE have a great deal to be thankful for," the old mouse had been remarking to his better-half the morning of the very day on which the appalling question of "getting a cat" had been discussed, "the absence of some one who shall be nameless makes up for much. On the whole I don't see that we should be likely to mend matters by changing our quarters."

"Certainly not, in *my* humble opinion," put in Flip, with a jerk of his distinguished tail. "I am really in a position to advise you, my dear father, from my intimacy with our benefactress, Poppy. So long as we conduct ourselves as wellbred mice always prefer to do, we have no reason for uneasiness."

Father Bright-eyes looked at his eldest son admiringly.

"How he expresses himself," he thought. "He is really a mouse any parents might be proud of. Take him altogether—the twist in his tail is of course a great natural advantage—but take him altogether we have not done so badly by him, my dear," he observed to Mrs. Bright-eyes, when sure that Flip was out of hearing. For he was far too sensible, of course, to praise him to his face. "I am not at all surprised that Poppy, as he calls her, should have taken him under her special protection."

The spring was coming on by now. Already some baskets of primroses had found their way down the street where Jack and Bessie and Poppy lived, and one day when, as usual, the opposite neighbours were having a little talk while waiting for the perambulator, Jack stuffed a tiny bunch of violets into the small caretaker's hands.

"My!" she exclaimed, poking her round nose into the middle of the posy, "but they do smell sweet. Thank you kindly, Master Jack. Has they come from the country, should you think now, from the real country?" and her eyes sparkled.

Signs of Spring

"To be sure," Jack replied. "We'll bring you more next week, Poppy. We're going to the country to spend the day on our birthday."

"We've got the same birthday," said Bessie. "Isn't it funny? though Jack's seven and I'm only six. We have a treat every birthday—a treat and a wish—the treat's to be going to the country, but we haven't fixed the wish yet."

But Poppy could only repeat, "Going to the country, the real country. You'll tell me all about it, master and missy, won't you?"

"Of course. But we've often been there. We go every year. Have you never been in the country, Poppy?"

Poppy shook her head.

"Never as I can remember," she said. "Mother's going to take me some day, though, only it won't be till she's saved a good bit. Do them flowers," and she pointed to the violets, "do they grow always? and the primroses?—I'd dearly love to see 'em all a-growing."

"They only grow in the spring," said Bessie. "At least—at least the primroses. I'm not quite sure about the violets," and she looked at Jack. But Jack was too wise to commit himself. "Poor Poppy, I wish you could come to the country in the spring."

The two children walked away rather more slowly and seriously than usual this morning. It had never come home to them quite so closely how others—children of their own age—have to "do without." And the day that this *does* come home to us is a marked one in our lives. Marked in a very blessed way if it leads to doing, as well as feeling.

"Jack," said Bessie after a while. "I think my birthday wish is beginning to get fixed. Is yours?"

"I—I almost think so too," said Jack

"I *had* thought of a doll's dinner-service," said Bessie with a slight quiver in her voice.

"And I *was* thinking of a winding-up steam-engine," said Jack rather gruffly.

And then for a day or two they said no more about it.

Mammas of all ranks, I think, must be pretty well used to being surprised. Children would not be children, and certainly much less nice than they are, if one always knew or at least had a very good idea of what they were going to do or say. But Jack's and Bessie's Mamma was rather *extra* surprised when, a few days before the double birthday, the two children came to tell her they had fixed what their wish was to be, and that it was "to take Poppy with us to the country."

"To take whom?" asked Mamma, hastily running over in her mind all the individuals, dog, cat, toy-horse, or doll, that "Poppy" could possibly be.

"She's the little caretaker at No. 9, and she's never seen the country, not to say to remember it. And her mother goes out charing, and her real name's Sleena Mary," Bessie ran off glibly.

Mamma looked aghast.

"My dear Bessie, what has nurse been thinking of?" she exclaimed, getting up as she spoke. But Jack and Bessie pulled her back.

"Oh, Mamma dear, it's no harm. Don't be vexed with nurse. We've only talked to her a little, and she told us about the mice, and she's *very* good. You would see she's good," they intreated. So Mamma sat down again and listened to the whole, and her face grew kinder and kinder, as Bessie nudged Jack to observe, especially when they came to the part of Poppy's longing to see primroses really a-growing. And the kind look grew more than kind when the two Jacks-in-the-middle explained that the "wish" was not to cost them nothing, but was to be at the price of the self-acting steam-engine and the lovely doll's dinner-service. Only being a prudent Mamma as well as a kind one, all she would *promise* was to see and think about it

CHAPTER VI.

FAIRYLAND.

THE very next day Poppy's mother, who happened to be at home, had a visitor—a visitor so gentle and friendly and sympathizing that her whole simple story, from the old days of "when father was alive and we lived in the country" to the present good-luck of "a winter rent-free," was soon told. And Poppy's—that is to say "Sleena Mary's"—small womanly ways and funny fancies, brought smiles to the visitor's face.

"Never was such a child for amusin' of herself," said the mother. "She'll be goin' to school again, but I had to keep her at home a bit this winter, for her eyes was weakly and the doctor wouldn't let her read. But she's better now—the good air of this fine house's set her up."

"It seems a nice house," said the children's mother, "and you keep it so tidy."

"It's nice and clean all over. The old people as lived here was very pertickler, and Poppy's always a-keeping down the dust," said the caretaker with pride. And she was very proud to show the lady through the rooms.

"It is a very nice house," she repeated as she went. And to herself she added—"I think it would be the very thing for *them* if they decide upon taking a house, and it would be nice to have them so near." The long-looked-for birthday fell on a Wednesday. People are fond of saying that things very seldom turn out as we wish them in this world, and perhaps in some ways this is true. Still I have noticed that sometimes, and especially when really good and kind and nice wishes are concerned, things do often turn out very right indeed. That was the case this time. Though only April, the most fickle of months, the day was lovely, quite lovely; the sort of day on which you could *feel* that the birds and the flowers and the squirrels and the rabbits, with thoughts of which little Poppy's head was stuffed full, must be all enjoying themselves thoroughly. And never

Down The Lane did children's faces look brighter and happier than those of our three little friends, as under the safe care of Nurse No. 2, they drove off in the brougham, which Papa had said they must have for the occasion to the railway. The baby brothers kissed their hands from the nursery window, Mamma called after them that they must look out for their cousin at the station, and Poppy's mother stood, curtseying and smiling at the area gate of No 9, hardly able to believe she was not dreaming.

And even the Bright-eyes family had no reason to grudge Poppy her treat, for she had begged her mother to put some crumbs in the usual place for them.

An hour and a half brought the travellers to their journey's end. By this time Poppy was almost speechless with delight. The first real green fields and woods had been met by her with cries of pleasure, but when, as they went further, the country grew still prettier, and here and there on the banks the yellow primroses smiled up in welcome and the birds flitted about in the sunshine, she grew silent.

"Don't you like it, Poppy?" asked Bessie.

"Bless you, missy, I should rather think I did. I've no more words to say—that's what it is," she answered.

She found her tongue again however when they had got out of the train and were walking through the lanes with the cousin who had come to meet them with her nurse.

"Shall we go home by the lane and the fields?" asked Delia. "Won't Poppy like it better than the road?"

For the Jacks-in-the-middles' Mamma had written all about Poppy, and Delia meant to join her cousins in making the little caretaker's first day in the country as happy as possible.

"Of course she would, and so would we," said Bessie. "It's such fun climbing stiles after you've been a good long while in London."

"And this afternoon we are to go to the wood to get primroses for auntie," said Delia. "She wrote that she wanted a lot for a dinner-party. Mamma will lend us her nice flat flower-baskets—we line them with damp moss and it keeps the flowers so much fresher than when they're all on the top of each other in deep baskets. If only it was warmer we might have had tea in the wood."

"Tea in the wood," repeated Poppy, in amazement.

Then they had to explain to her all about gipsy teas and picnics, and nutting and blackberrying expeditions, till the poor little girl became quite convinced that, as she told her mother that evening, Heaven itself couldn't be much beautifuller to live in than the country.

The whole day was to her a dream of delight, and I am quite sure that the sight of her pleasure had a good deal to do with Jack's and Bessie's conviction that this was the happiest birthday they had ever had.

They were all at the primrose gathering when they arrived at this conclusion. They had had a very good dinner indeed in Delia's nursery, and Poppy had had dinner with them.

"For you see, auntie," said Bessie, when Delia's mother had

consulted her and nurse on this knotty point, "it wouldn't seem so like treating her as a friend if we sent her down to have her dinner

in the kitchen, would it? And very likely she'd be too shy to eat. She's not a bit shy with us, is she, Carter?"

"No, Miss Bessie, she seems to me just right, for she's not forward neither. She's really a very well-behaved little girl, ma'am," she added, to Delia's mother.

"So I think," she replied.

THROUGH THE FIELDS

They lent Poppy a basket, so that she might fill it herself with primroses for her mother.

"Won't she just be pleased?" she said. "She does so love the country. Does these beautiful flowers grow always here, Miss?"

"Oh no, only in the spring," Bessie replied. "But in summer there's lots of other kinds—honeysuckle and dog-roses and wild hyacinths and—and—oh lots, But I don't think any are as pretty as the spring ones; do you, Delia?"

"I don't know," Delia replied. "Perhaps it seems so because we're so pleased to see them after the winter. "Hush," she cried suddenly, "be quite quiet—there's a field-mouse—don't you see? there under the leaves. Oh, it's gone! I do so like them; they have such bright eyes."

Poppy gazed before her in astonishment.

"A field-mouse," she said. "Is there mice as lives in the country, just like there's people as lives there?"

All the other children laughed.

"Yes, of course," they said.

"I wish I'd seen him," she said. "That'll be something to tell Flip about, next time he comes for his dinner," she added to herself. "Poor Flip! I wish I could have brought him to see the country too."

CHAPTER VII.

A MOUSE CONCLAVE.

THE happy day came to an end at last, as all days both happy and sad do. But in one way it did not come to an end: indeed its pleasure lasted on for a good many other days to come, for Poppy especially — the telling mother all about it was so delightful.

And another pair of ears besides mother's took it in too. Flip was there, in a corner of the kitchen where no one saw him, listening eagerly. He had missed Poppy the day before, and a great deal of curiosity had been felt by all the Bright-eyes family as to what had become of her, and Flip had run out into the kitchen extra early that morning to find out if she had come back again.

No, Poppy was not there, only her mother who seemed very busy cooking something—*was* she cooking? thought Flip—on the dresser. It must be something very nice, surely; she had such a pleased smile on her thin face. He waited till she went into the next room, a nice airy room behind the kitchen where she and her little daughter slept, and then like a flash of lightning he was up on the top of the dresser, peering about with his gleaming black eyes, snuffing about with his sharp little nose, in search of the wonderful dish which had so absorbed the caretaker's attention. There was nothing to smell, *almost* nothing at least, only a faint, fresh perfume which Flip had never come in contact with before, and to *see*, why what was that? A round flat dish, an old soup-plate in fact, filled almost to the outside edge with pale yellow blossoms, bordered by soft green leaves, which Poppy's mother had carefully set round them as a frame. Flip did not call them blossoms and leaves; poor Flip, in spite of his ancestral tail and his cleverness, he was only a town mouse, he had never seen the fields and the hedges and had no wish to do so!

"Funny looking things," he said to himself, "they have almost no scent, and I don't *think* they can be good to eat."

He was stepping cautiously along the edge, for he was sharp enough to descry water not far off.

"Let's see," and he nibbled one delicate petal. "Faugh! Horrid,

FLIP TASTES THE PRIMROSE'S

tasteless stuff, what in the world was the silly old woman looking so delighted at?"

Just then Poppy and her mother came into the kitchen; Flip hastily decamped to a shady corner, but not before the caretaker had caught sight of his tail.

"I declare," she said, "if that isn't owdacious! one of those mice of yours, Poppy, a'sniffin at the primroses."

"Oh don't touch him, mother," cried the little girl anxiously, not that there was any fear truly of the caretaker's being able to do so! "It's Flip, I'm sure; I dare say he knows I've been in the country. I'm not sure if I told him, but he may have heard us talking about it."

Flip smiled to himself in his corner, and decided to stay and hear more. But Poppy's mother looked at her rather anxiously: the little girl was rubbing her eyes and her rosy face looked drowsy though smiling.

"My deary, you've not had your sleep out, you're dreaming still," she said.

Poppy shook her head.

"No, I'm not indeed," she said. But seeing that her mother seemed uneasy, she said no more about Flip and his family. "Shall I go on telling you about it all yesterday, mother dear?" she said. "You like that better than my mouse stories, don't you? But there's mice in the country too, did you know that? just as there is children in the town and children in the country, you know, mother. It do seem quite natural-like, don't it?"

"Field-mice is not quite the same kind, I don't think," said her mother. "And children is children all the world over, I take it."

"No, no, mother, you're wrong there," said Poppy brightly, "and I can prove it you. Many a time you've said to me I was more like a country-child than a town-child, 'cos of my rosy cheeks. There now, mother."

They had a laugh over this, and then Poppy went on with her glowing account of all she had seen and done the day before, finishing up with the old wish.

"Oh, mother, if we could but go and live in the country like we used to when I was a baby!"

And Flip listened too, with all his ears.

There was a great discussion that evening in the nest of the Bright-eyes family. It is at night, as perhaps you know, that mice are at their best and sharpest, so all questions of importance among them are talked over when we, tail-less, two-legged beings are asleep and dreaming, and Flip waited till night to tell his father and mother and brothers and sisters of all the wonderful things he had been hearing, and to propose that they should all as a family emigrate to the country.

But Papa shook his head. He thought his son very sharp and clever, but still—" there is a very great deal to consider and inquire about," he said, "a very great deal. First and foremost what about," and he glanced cautiously round, "about the nameless one in the strange land you speak of?"

ONE OF THE NAMELESS ONES

"There was no mention of her," exclaimed Flip eagerly. "I fancy none of that race have found their way there."

"It is to be hoped so," returned Mr. Bright-eyes solemnly. "But furthermore, my son, what are the resources of the country? Is there cake? Is there biscuit? Are there even such common necessaries as bread-crumbs and cheese?"

Flip hesitated, he had not gone into all these matters of detail as yet; no doubt the cousins of whom Poppy had spoken, would furnish them with all information. But here his Mamma interrupted. She did not feel too sure on that point; there were cousins

"WE WILL NOT DESERT NUMBER NINE"

and cousins, and these country cousins were but distant connections. She remembered, but vaguely only, having heard of them in her young mousehood, but certainly not as *near* relatives. Flip began to feel rather small; suddenly a bright idea struck him.

"Permit me, my dear parents," he said. "I do not see that any of the objections you have urged are very important, though of course they should be considered. But a new reflection strikes me, which I fear good feeling will force us to give in to. However greatly to our advantage it might be to emigrate, what of our benefactors and friends, Poppy and her mother! Would it not be too ungrateful, too heartless of us to leave them? Think of Poppy's distress!" here his voice broke and his emotion spread to the others. The whole family wept silently. "No, no," Flip continued, "we cannot think of it. I withdraw my proposal. For Poppy's sake, for dear Poppy's sake the Bright-eyes family will not desert No. 9."

"Hear, hear," exclaimed the five other voices, "bravo, Flip, for Poppy's sake we will not desert No. 9."

CHAPTER VIII.

POPPY GIVES AND TAKES ADVICE.

POPPY was sitting alone in the kitchen the next afternoon—that is to say the afternoon but one after the birthday treat—at her knitting as usual. Her mother was out, but she had promised to be home by tea-time.

"I wish she would come," thought the little girl. "I've several more things to tell her that I'd forgotten. How nice it would be to be living somewhere where mother didn't need to go out all day and leave me alone; I'll be glad to go back to school again," and she gave a little sigh. "I wonder what Master Jack and Miss Bessie are doin' to-day. They said they'd come over to see me soon, but of course they've got their lessons to do and a many other things, and it'd never do, as mother says, for me to put myself for'ard too much, though they've been so wonderful good to me."

She was feeling a little dull after the great excitement of the birthday treat, and perhaps she was still rather tired with the railway and the exercise in the fresh air, all so unusual in her quiet life. The knitting-needles dropped from her hands, her little round head fell back against the rail of the high, old-fashioned rocking-chair, and Poppy was fast asleep.

Suddenly—she sat straight up with a start—something had touched her foot, nay, something was moving right up her leg and—lo! and behold—a pair of bright eyes were staring up in her face. Flip, tail and all, was sitting on her knee! For half an instant Poppy felt inclined to scream. Even if one is on very friendly terms with mice one doesn't *quite* like to feel them running over one. But before she had time to get her breath for even the tiniest cry, a little voice stopped her.

"Forgive me, dear Poppy, I beg of you," it said. "I would not have taken such a liberty as to run up your leg, had not all other means of attracting your attention failed."

"Dear me," thought Poppy, "how very grandly he talks! I wonder if he goes to school now and learns all those long words there?" But as she was afraid of hurting Flip's feelings she did not say this aloud.

"Never mind," she replied. "I didn't like it much when I felt you on my legs, but if you'll sit still now and not flop about your long tail I dare say I'll get used to you. Why haven't you been to see me for so long—though to be sure," she added, with considerable pride, "I've been away—you didn't know, did you, that I'd been in the country—ever so far?"

Flip gave a superior smile, but I am afraid it was lost on Poppy. It takes a good deal of education to see when a mouse is smiling.

"Oh dear, yes," he said, "I know all about it. I ventured to listen to all you were telling your good mother yesterday, and it gave me great food for thought. In fact—I particularly wanted to tell you about it, that was why I intruded this afternoon—we had a very serious discussion last night as to whether we, the Bright-eyes family, might not do well to emigrate ourselves to the country. Hearing of our cousins still being there made us feel we should not be without friends; and there seem to be other advantages. You—you do not appear to have come across any member of the —the family who shall be nameless?" he added, dropping his voice and speaking rather nervously.

Poppy did not immediately reply.

"I'd really like to put him down a little," she said to herself, "he *is* so affected. Well," she added aloud, "and when are you thinking of starting—all six of you, I suppose? And how do you mean to get there? And how would you like sleeping out in the fields and hedges, where it's pretty cold very often I dare say, you that's used to a nice warm kitchen! And how would you do without the scraps and crumbs *we* give you; I suppose you think you'd get better fare from your grand-cousins—eh?"

Flip looked very reproachful.

"Poppy," he said, "you might listen to all I have to tell you. We decided against it. I proposed and it was unanimously agreed that—" and here Flip's feelings became too much for him, he lifted up one paw and wiped his right eye, "that it would be—would be *ungrateful*, Poppy, ungrateful to you and to your good mother who have been kind friends to us, to leave you. No, Poppy, we do not deserve your sharp words—we decided that we would not desert No. 9."

Poppy's tender heart was touched at once.

"Poor Flip," she exclaimed, "I'm very sorry if I've hurt your feelings. But I'm very glad you've given up the idea, for though I wouldn't have mentioned it if you hadn't asked me—for I know you don't like talking about it—at Miss Delia's house, Miss Delia's own cousin to Master Jack and Miss Bessie over the way, and it was her Mamma's house we went to, so I know all about it, well, at her house there's a *very* big, *very* big—I think they call her a Pushon—or some name like that, a *very* big c—"

"Stop! stop! oh stop! Poppy," cried Flip, and Poppy could see that he was trembling all over, "do not, I entreat of you do not say the word. How thankful, oh how thankful I am that we gave up the idea!"

"Yes, indeed, and so you may be," said Poppy. "For I rather fancy there's more c—— more of them about. There's stables you know, and all sorts of farm places, and there's sure to be—"

"Say no more," sighed Flip. "Ah, how I pity our poor cousins!"

Poppy looked puzzled.

"I don't think field-mice are the same," she said. "They live out-of-doors altogether you see—but *you* couldn't do that, Flip, you'd die of cold. Best let well alone."

Just then the door was heard to open; the caretaker was coming in. Off darted Flip, and Poppy sat up and rubbed her eyes. "My deary, have you been taking a nap?" said her mother.

"I don't know," Poppy replied. And after a minute she spoke again, "Mother," she said, "is it wrong of me to want so to go to live in the country? Is it best to be pleased always to stay where one is?"

"It's best to do one's duty, and things gets clear as one goes on," said her mother. "Don't think too much about it, deary.

"It's best to do one's duty"

If it came in our way to go back to live in the country, as *was* our home you may say, we'd be very happy I make no doubt. But frettin' for a thing one can't have is wrong. Do your duty and trust as we won't be forgotten. That's what I says to myself," said the poor woman.

And then Poppy and her mother had a cheerful tea together.

CHAPTER IX.

BAD NEWS.

A DAY or two after Poppy's conversation with Flip, there came a particularly bright and sunny morning. Such mornings, in London especially, are rare in early spring-time.

"It does one good to see the sun shining so," said the caretaker, as she set off on a day's charing. "You might bring your work and sit on the top of the area steps a bit, Poppy, if you put your little shawl on, after you've tidied up."

"Yes, mother, and may be I'll see Master Jack and Miss Bessie if they pass. Such a fine morning they're pretty sure to be goin' out a walk early," the little girl replied.

She was not mistaken. Just about eleven o'clock when she

and her knitting needles were comfortably settled on the top step, the door of the house opposite opened and the usual little party sallied forth. Jack and Bessie were across the street in an instant.

"Good morning, Poppy," they both exclaimed. "We've been so wanting to see you. Were you very tired the day after our birthday?"

"I was a bit sleepy," Poppy answered, her round face broadening out into a smile, "but what did that matter? Oh, Miss Bessie, but it was a beautiful day! I'll never forget it—no, never. I've been wantin' dreadful to see you to tell you again how I did enjoy it!"

"I *am* so glad you did," exclaimed Bessie, and Jack joined in of course.

"You'll have some more treats like it some day p'r'aps," said he in his slow way. He was not near so quick as Bessie, though he was a year older. "When we go to the country—we always do, you know, about July or August, isn't it, Bessie?—we're going to ask Mamma for you to come there, aren't we, Bessie?"

"Oh, I do hope it'll be in my holidays," said Poppy, clasping her hands together." Do you think it will, miss? For I'm goin' to school again now reg'lar. I'm to begin on Monday."

But their plans were just then interrupted by the voice of the under-nurse who had joined them. She had got little Leonard, the baby but one, by the hand this morning, for it was so fine and dry nurse thought it would do him good to walk, and *the* baby was having an extra long sleep, and was not therefore ready to come out so early.

"Is your mother in, Poppy?" Carter asked, and on the child shaking her head, "Will she be in to-morrow?" the nurse went on, "No, I don't mean to-morrow, for that's Sunday, Monday, I should say?"

"Yes," Poppy went on, "sure to be. She ain't a goin' out so much now, for you see I'm goin' to school, and it don't do to leave the house too much. Yes, I know mother'll be in all Monday."

"That's all right then," said Carter. "I had a sort of message for her, but if she's to be in on Monday, there's no need to explain. It'll be all right."—"The child wouldn't understand, the ladies will tell her mother themselves," thought the nurse to herself, in which she made a mistake, not knowing how very "understanding" Poppy was. And this mistake of hers caused a good deal of sorrow that might have been avoided.

Then the children bade their little friend good-bye and went on for their walk, leaving her with new fancies out of which to spin pleasant day-dreams.

"To go down to see them in the country again," thought Poppy. "Oh, I do hope it'll be in my holidays. I'll work my best at school, that I will, so as I'll deserve a treat if it comes, as mother says."

And full of these good resolutions, the little maiden set off for school on Monday morning. She was a favourite there, for she was both quick and willing, and she was pleased to find herself put back in her former place, even though she had been three months absent.

"You were well on for your age before you were away, Selina," the teacher said. "I should be sorry to put you back. If you can work a little extra at home for a week or two, I think you may keep up. Your eyes are quite well again?"

"Yes, ma'am, only mother won't let me use 'em much by candlelight. I do my knitting mostly of an evening."

"That's right. But the days are getting longer now. You'll have plenty of time by daylight for all you need to do."

Swinging her bag of books little Poppy ran cheerily home. It was nice to know mother would be there. What had the nurse asked if she'd be in for? she wondered. She had forgotten about it till now, and she had not told her mother. But the nurse had said it didn't matter—perhaps it was just that Bessie's Mamma was coming over to speak to the charwoman, as she had done before.

Yes, mother was there; the door was opened as soon as Poppy knocked. And mother smiled and listened to all the child had to tell, so that for a moment or two, Poppy did not notice that she was pale and her eyes rather red, as if she had been crying a little. But as soon as she did see it she flew to her mother and kissed her.

"Is there anything the matter? Are you ill, dear mother?" she asked anxiously.

"No, no, deary," said the poor woman, trying to smile and checking back the tears, "it's downright ongrateful of me, it is, to make a trouble of what was bound to come. I should be thankful for the good its done us, you 'specially, Poppy. You're not to say the same child as when we came here, and—"

Poppy's rosy face grew pale too.

"I know," she said, "the house is took."

Her mother answered more brightly,

"Not to say *took*, but it looks like it," she said. "But, Poppy love, we mustn't make a trouble of it, we mustn't indeed. There's been some ladies to look at it, and by all I could hear they liked it very much and said it seemed just the thing. They were very civil to me and give me a shilling for my trouble—real ladies they was. But of course I couldn't have axed no questions as to when it'd be for, and such-like. We'll just have to cheer-up and make the best of it. I'll step round to the agent's in a few days,

"I KNOW SHE SAID 'THE HOUSE IS TOOK'!"

if I don't hear nothing, and find out, and if it's got to be, we must look out for a nice little room again, or maybe two."

"Will you go back to Smith Street, do you think, mother?" asked Poppy in a voice which she vainly tried to keep from trembling.

The caretaker shook her head.

"I don't think Smith Street was healthy," she said. "No, I'll try and find somewhere nicer. And who knows—I might get another house to keep. The agent knows I'm trusty and careful."

"But not far from here, mother," said Poppy. "I'd never see Master Jack and Miss Bessie if it was far."

Her mother promised to do her best. But they were both very sad, poor things. Curiously enough Poppy never thought again of the nurse's undelivered message—it never struck her that it could have anything to do with the visit of the stranger ladies to see the house.

CHAPTER X.

DELIA'S BIG SISTER.

A FEW days went on and nothing was heard by Poppy and her mother about the house being taken. They were almost beginning to hope that it had been a false alarm, for "there's many a slip 'twixt the cup and the lip," said the caretaker, who was rather fond of proverbs, when one morning, just as Poppy was coming in from school, there appeared a man sent by the agent to take down the board announcing that the "desirable residence was to be sold or let."

"And you'll clean off the paper in the front window too, please," said the young man, civilly enough, as he was leaving.

"Then it's quite true — the house is really taken?" she said.

"Certainly it is," he replied, "and a good job too for the owners."

"To be sure," she said, trying to smile, "what's one man's meat is another man's poison," which the agent thought rather a good joke.

"You don't know as your gentleman is in want of a caretaker for any other house, do you?" she said timidly.

"Can't say, I'm sure. But there's houses dropping in every day. T'would do no harm for you to step round and ask for yourself. And oh, by the by, I was forgetting I was to tell you you needn't turn out till you hear more. The party that's taken the house might want you to stay on a bit when their things begin to come in—"

"When are they coming?"

"They want to be in and settled by the middle of May," he said. "You'll come in for the cleaning-down, maybe. You see there's not much painting or papering needed; it's in such good condition."

And with these words he took his departure.

Considering what he had told her, Poppy's mother thought it best not to "step round" to the agent's.

"They might think me a worrit," she said to her little daughter, "seein' as how they've already spoke for me to the gentlefolk as has bought the house. We must just wait a bit, Poppy, and see."

SHE INQUIRED AMONG HER FORMER NEIGHBOURS

All the same, without saying anything to her little daughter, she inquired among some of her former neighbours about a room in some decent locality in case nothing else in the way of caretaking turned up. She had been out on this errand the following Wednesday afternoon, Poppy's half-holiday, leaving the little girl in charge—Poppy only thought that her mother had been out shopping—so as the caretaker came near to number nine on her return, she was surprised to see the child looking out for her with evident eagerness.

"Nothing wrong, deary?" she said cheerfully, though with a little sinking at her heart. Her small "house hunting" on her own account had not tended to raise her spirits; she minded nothing for herself, but for Poppy! The few rooms within her means seemed sadly poor and stuffy; surely the rents had gone up even in the last few months? "nothing wrong?" she repeated. Supposing the new owners of the house were coming in at once, and did not want her at all?

"No, no, mother, at least I don't think so. The ladies, at least one of them, has been here; it was quite a young lady; she came to take a measure for her Mamma she said, and oh! just fancy, mother, she was Miss Delia's—Miss Delia-in-the-country's big sister! She's stayin' over the way, and she knowed me—she said, 'Well, my little girl, and how have you been getting on?'"

Poppy's mother was very much interested.

"I wish I could see some of the ladies," she said. "They'd maybe speak a word for me for the cleaning."

"If Miss Delia had been there I could have said somethin' about it," Poppy added. "If only I wasn't at school all day, mother, I'd have ever so much more chance of seein' Master Jack and Miss

"I SAW THE LITTLE GIRL— I FORGET HER NAME."

Bessie. I'm sure they'll be sorry when we go away from this house; they're real kind, and so's their Mamma."

"But if so be as it's their cousins as is comin', they'll be pleased at that too," said her mother. "Goods and bads is queerly mixed up in this world. Any way I'm right down glad you had your day in the country with an easy mind, my deary."

Over the way in Jack's and Bessie's home the same subject, little as Poppy and her mother suspected it, was being talked about.

"I saw the little girl—I forget her name—the caretaker's little girl at number nine, Auntie, when I went over there to measure the drawing-room mantelpiece for mother," said Constance, Delia's "big sister," as Poppy had described her.

Her aunt started.

"Oh, by the by, I meant to have gone over to speak to the poor woman. I did send a message by Carter to tell her not to be uneasy. But it was difficult for me to know what to say till your mother had seen her for herself."

"But Mamma did see her for herself, the other day you know, when she came to look over the house," said Constance. "Didn't she tell her then what we've been thinking of?"

"No, several things had to be considered first and some inquiries made. It was only yesterday I heard that your father and mother had decided to offer her the lodge. I quite meant to have gone over to speak to her, but I have been so exceedingly busy. However she is a sensible woman, and she must have had my message. I'll go over this afternoon."

"Yes, do," said Constance. "Somehow I don't feel sure—the poor little girl did look rather melancholy now I come to think of it."

But the afternoon was already well advanced, and before the children's mother could start some callers came, who stayed so long that by the time they left it was decidedly too late. Her visit had to be put off till the next morning.

And all this time Poppy's heart was very sore. She did not like to say much to her mother who was sad enough already. She was not sorry that evening to catch sight of a small dark object in one corner of the kitchen, which crept towards her when she called it gently.

"Flip, Flip," she said, "come and speak to me. Mother's in the back kitchen washing. "Oh, Flip, have you heard that we're going away—that the house is taken?"

"I thought something was the matter," Flip replied. "I—I could not help hearing some conversation between you and your mother. It is very distressing, just too when we had given up all idea of emigrating, for your sake, dear Poppy. I fear I could not persuade my parents to change their minds again about going to the country."

"But *we're* not going there—I wish we were! Only you didn't give up for our sakes only, Flip—you know what I told you about the c—"

Flip shivered.

"Hush!" he said. "Yes, that is true certainly. But it is a sad look-out. Who knows what sort of people the newcomers may be, or *who*," and here his voice dropped, "*who* may come with them?"

"Poor Flip!" said Poppy, "yes, it's very sad for all of you too. But I'll tell you what—I know the ladies who are coming

"Flip, Flip. Come and speak to me."

—I'll see if I can't get them to promise not to have a—you know what. You be sure to come and have another talk with me before we go, and I'll tell you if I've been able to ask them."

"Oh, thank you, dear Poppy, thank you," said Flip. "I'll—" but at that moment the charwoman came in, and off he scudde tail and all!

CHAPTER XI.

ALMOST TOO GOOD TO BE TRUE.

"GOOD morning, Mrs. Orchard." (I don't think I have ever mentioned that Poppy's last name was Orchard, have I? A nice country-sounding name it is, isn't it?) "I am so sorry not to have come over to see you before, but you got my nurse's message?" said Bessie's mother to Poppy's, the next day when she found herself at last standing at the door of number nine opposite.

The caretaker stared.

"No, ma'am, I don't think I've had any message," she said. "And if it was given to Poppy, she's a thinkin' kind of child; she wouldn't go to forget to tell me. She's just in from school, ma'am, I'll call her. But would you kindly step down to the kitchen, there's not a chair nor a stool anywhere else, though it won't be long like that. You've heard, ma'am, as the house is taken?"

She was rather excited at the lady's visit and it made her talk more than usual, as she led the way to the kitchen, Bessie's mother following her.

"Yes," she replied, "it is about that I wanted to speak to you, and it will take some little time to explain, so we may as well sit down and talk comfortably. Oh, here is Poppy. How are you, my dear? Didn't my second nurse give you a message from me for your mother the other day, Poppy?"

Poppy considered.

"No, ma'am," she replied, "she only asked me if mother would be in on Monday, and I said I knew she would be. Perhaps I should have told mother, but I never thought of it again."

"You should 'a told me," said the caretaker.

"Oh, but that wasn't the message," said the lady. "There must have been some mistake about it. My message was to tell you, Mrs. Orchard, that the ladies who were coming to see the house were relations of ours, and that you mustn't be put out about having to leave, as we should think of you in making our plans. I must speak to Carter about it."

The poor woman's face cleared.

"And I'm sure, ma'am, it was very kind of you to think of us. If maybe I might make so bold, I'd be proud to do the cleaning and see to the furniture a bit when it comes in. It'd give me nice time to look about for a new place for us."

"Certainly," her visitor replied. "I've no doubt my sister would be glad to keep you on here a little. But I have much more to speak of than that. How would you and Poppy like to go to the country to live, Mrs. Orchard? The smaller of the two lodges at my sister's, the place Poppy was at on their birthday with the children, is empty, and they want some one for it. There is not so much gate opening as at the principal lodge, and it is close to the farm and not lonely: it is a pretty little house, and you would have it rent-free and a few shillings a week, and you might take in some washing."

She was half surprised when she stopped speaking that there was no reply. But glancing up, she quickly saw the reason: the tears were streaming down the poor woman's face; she *could* not speak while little Poppy's cheeks were crimson with excitement and her eyes dancing in her head.

"Oh! mother, mother," she cried, "don't take on so. Do tell the lady as it'll be like heaven to us to go and live in the country, oh, mother, do!"

A SHUDDER WENT THROUGH THE GROUP OF BRIGHTEYES.

Mrs. Orchard choked down her tears.

"Oh, ma'am," she said. "Indeed what she says is true. I don't know where to find words for to thank you, for it's all come of your goodness to us. I do trust as I'll show I'm grateful by doing all in my power to serve your friends faithful."

"I'm sure you will," said Jack's and Bessie's mother kindly,—there were tears in her own eyes, I fancy,—" and I am so glad you like the idea. My sister will be here herself next week, and she will come in and see you and talk it all over. Her eldest daughter is here now."

"Yes'm," said Poppy. "I saw it was Miss Delia's big sister, and mother and me we hoped as maybe 'twas your ladies that were takin' the house, because of the cleanin' you see; but we never thought of anything like *this!*" and the child quite gasped with her delight.

"There's only one thing, ma'am, no — there's two things," she went on confidingly. Poppy was not

I'll tell Flip what you say, ma'am.

a shy child. "I'll be so sorry not to see Master Jack and Miss Bessie," and her pretty blue eyes grew tearful.

"But you will see them, my dear," said the lady. "They very often go out to their aunt's, and sometimes they stay there several weeks. It is only for a short time of the year that my relations are to be in London, you know."

Poppy grew quite bright again.

"That will be nice," she said, "and to be sure it isn't as if mother and me had been going to stay here in this house, we might have been several streets off."

"And what is the other thing?" asked the children's mother. "You said there were two?"

Poppy grew very red.

"It's—it's only—p'r'aps I might ask the ladies when they come themselves," she said at last. "It's only—I do *ope* they won't keep a cat."

She fancied she heard a slight rustle in a corner of the kitchen, for Poppy was very quick of hearing. She was right; six pairs of long little ears were eagerly listening for the lady's reply.

"A cat," she repeated, looking puzzled—oh, dear, what a shudder went through the group of Bright-eyes standing at the door of their hole!

"Why shouldn't they keep a cat, my dear?"

"Oh, ma'am, Poppy's quite silly-like about the mice," said her mother apologetically. "There's some here that's so tame, she's come quite to make pets of 'em. They do no harm, I'll say that for them, and there don't seem many."

"Only Flip—and the father and mother," said Poppy glibly.

The lady could not help smiling.

"Are these your names for them?" she said. "Well, now I come to think of it, I dare say my friends will not keep a cat, for the girls have some very favourite birds. But you'd better ask them yourself, Poppy, when you see them next week, and perhaps you might say a word or two for your pet mice. If they promise to be very good and not mischievous, and if no other mice come to live at number nine, perhaps my sister will allow this family to stay here unmolested. There are mice and mice, you know; some are exceedingly tiresome and mischievous."

"Ours aren't like that, I'm sure," answered Poppy. "All the same I'll tell Flip," and seeing the amused glances between the lady and her mother she blushed a little. "I'll tell Flip what you say, ma'am. And when Miss Delia's Mamma comes I'll ask her. I am so glad they don't like cats."

Soon after this, Jack's and Bessie's mother went away, Mrs. Orchard and Poppy following her with their smiling faces to the door.

"It is a real pleasure to see them looking so happy," thought the kind lady to herself.

And oh, what a joyful afternoon the two had; talking over the news that seemed almost too good to be true, picturing the little cottage to themselves, planning what new things they would be able to buy to make it look pretty and neat. "For we must be a credit to the ladies, you see, Poppy," said her mother.

CHAPTER XII.

DELIA'S DREAM.

BRIGHT, warm, lovely summer! If spring, early spring even, in the country, had seemed fairyland to little Poppy, what words could she find for these blue and golden days, with their wealth of flowers and butterflies, birds singing overhead, sleepy-eyed cows in the fields, everything, so at least it seemed to her, fresh and sweet and happy! For it was a very lovely summer that year; such a summer as we cannot expect, in England at least, *always*.

"And it's the twentieth of July at last, mother," said the little girl, as she stood at the cottage door early that morning, "and they're really coming this afternoon, Master Jack and Miss Bessie, as well as our own ladies. Isn't it funny that Miss Delia and Miss Constance and their Mamma should be our ladies, more than Miss Bessie and her Mamma? I'll never feel as if they *were* more ours, mother, I'll never love *no* ladies—I mean *any* ladies—mother, teacher's very particular about my talkin', do you know?"

"And a very good thing. If you're ever to be a nurse to ladies' children as you want to be, Poppy, ladies think a deal about nice talking. I'm too old now to change myself, but I shall be pleased for you to learn to say the words right."

"Yes—I told teacher so," said Poppy, but she spoke rather absently. "Mother," she went on, "there's just one thing I'd like, to make me perfectly happy, if only the ladies were going to drive in at *our* gate, and me to open it!"

"Nobody can have everything," said her mother smiling. "But I tell you what—I do think we might both be standing near the big gates, to see them when they arrive. I know it'd be all right for me to lock up here just for once in a way."

Poppy flew to her mother and kissed her.

"Oh, yes, do let us," she said. "And p'r'aps Mr. Jemmit at the big lodge 'll let me help to open. He's rather stiff, you know, and the gates are very heavy. And oh, mother, you'll be sure to have the cakes and all for *beautiful* to-morrow, won't you? 'Thursday at five o'clock,' Miss Bessie wrote, 'we're all three coming to have tea with you and your mother, Poppy, in your new house.'" And Poppy was so happy that she was obliged to hop all round the kitchen and down the little garden path and back again, on one foot, to calm down her spirits a little.

"I wonder," she said presently, when she was sitting at breakfast with her mother, "I wonder if Miss Delia will bring all her birds down to the country. And if she does I do hope the servants at number nine won't go and get a cat, mother?"

Poppy looked quite distressed.

"There's no fear of their getting a cat so long as the mice do no mischief," said her mother. "There was no talk of it that time I went up for two nights to help when the cook was ill. Indeed the servants were saying it was a wonderful clear house for mice."

Poppy was so happy.

"I'm so glad. I do so hope Flip and all of them are very good," said Poppy, as if speaking to herself. "I'll ask Miss Delia all the same," she added.

And so she did, the next afternoon, when, as had been settled, the two girls and Jack came to take tea with Mrs. Orchard and Poppy.

What a happy tea-party it was! How the little guests praised the cakes and the jam—and the cream—which Poppy's mother had bought at the farm for a *great* treat—how pretty the neat table looked, with a clean cloth and a beautiful posy of the roses that grew round the lodge windows, in the middle! And after tea, when everybody declared they really *couldn't* eat any more, how Poppy did enjoy showing the children all over—besides the big kitchen there was a back one where Mrs. Orchard did all the cooking, so that the front room was as neat as a new pin always, and up stairs there was a nice big bedroom and a cosy tiny one out of it, which was to be Poppy's own when she was a big girl and able to earn money to furnish it. Then the bit of garden was a great source of pride, and a tiny wired-in poultry yard where they could keep a few hens and have fresh eggs to sell and sometimes to eat—all had to be shown, and the little guests took as much interest in it as if it were their own.

"To think of it all coming of Jack's and my having colds and looking out of the nursery window to amuse ourselves! When I saw you at the lodge yesterday afternoon, Poppy, I said to Delia it was really like a story, didn't I, Delia? Do you ever make up stories now, Poppy, about the mice, you know? How they must miss you at number nine!"

Poppy looked a little troubled.

"Miss Bessie," she said, "I didn't make up about Flip and the others. I might—*p'r'aps* I might have dreamed some of it, but not all. I'd have told you, I would indeed, if I had made it all up."

WHAT A HAPPY TEA PARTY IT WAS!

Bessie and Delia looked at each other and smiled.

"Tell her, Delia, do," said Bessie. "Listen, Poppy."

"It was about a dream *I* had," said Delia. "It was really very funny. It was the night before we left London. Everything was ready, all the trunks were packed—even a *mouse* might have had the sense to see we were going away, so that part of it one can understand. "Well, Poppy, I dreamt, or I didn't dream!—that a little dark mouse with a very long tail—"

"A tail with a twist at the end?" interrupted Poppy.

"Yes—I think so at least—well, he came on to my bed, I saw him plain against the white counterpane, and stood there quite still for a minute. Then I heard a little *teeny* voice say, 'Are you asleep, Miss Delia?' I was rather startled at first, but I answered 'No,' for whether I was asleep or not, I thought I was, you see. 'I beg your pardon,' he went on, 'for disturbing you at this unseasonable hour—' he did use such grand words!—but my excuse is that I may not have another opportunity. I see you are all going down to the country—we ourselves have often thought of taking a trip down there—we have cousins in the country, but for several reasons we have given up thoughts of it—and no doubt you will see our dear little friend, Poppy Orchard. May I ask you to give her my very kindest regards—Flip—Flip Bright-eyes is my name—and tell her we are all well, wonderfully well, and comfortable. We have kept to our part of the bargain, and you, Miss Delia, you and your kind Mamma have kept to yours. No—no nameless one has so far disturbed our peace of mind."

"'You mean we haven't any—' I was *just* going to say 'cat' when I remembered that in Poppy's sto—I mean Bessie told me that I mustn't say it to them—so I changed. '*I* certainly will never have any creature in the house who would hurt my birds, and so, Mr. Flip, I think you are all pretty safe as long as you all behave so well.' "He made a sort of twirl with his tail which I think was instead of a bow.

He made a sort of twirl with his tail

"'Thank you, thank you for the assurance,' he said. 'We are grateful, we are indeed. We never take anything we have no right to—not even a grain of bird-seed, unless it is on the floor—we find crumbs enough and to spare, thanks to your Mamma's liberality. Tell dear Poppy of our well-being and—' I don't know what more he was going to say, for just then mother came in with a candle to say good-night and off he scampered. But any way, dream or no dream, I have given you his message, Poppy."

Poppy had been listening with all her ears.

"I *am* glad of it," she said, "for many a time I've thought of poor Flip. Some day maybe, Miss Delia, I might have to go to help at number nine—and then I'd see Flip again. I'm *very* pleased he hasn't forgotten me."

The End

Lightning Source UK Ltd.
Milton Keynes UK
UKHW031010281022
411251UK00009B/566